Contents:

Acknowledgements	3

Section 1

Brief Introduction	4

Section 2

Authors Introduction	6

Section 3

Preparation for the Programme	11

Section 4

The Programme	13
Setting up a Counselling Service	22
The Wider School Context	33
Peer Buddying Pack - Involving the Students	38
Peer Buddying Programme - Residential	77

References and brief Bibliography	90
School of Emotional Literacy	92
Other Publications	93

First published in 2003 by The School of Emotional Literacy

This edition published in 2008 by Speechmark Publishing Ltd,
70 Alston Drive, Bradwell Abbey, Milton Keynes MK13 9HG
Tel: +44 (0) 1908 326944   Fax: +44 (0) 1908 326960

www.speechmark.net
www.schoolofemotional-literacy.com

Copyright © Emma Wills 2003

Emma Wills is hereby identified as the author of this work in accordance with Section 77 of the Copyright, Designs and Patents Act, 1988.

All rights reserved. Permission is gained for the user to photocopy or print out the worksheets. No other part of this publication may be reproduced or transmitted in any form or by any means, electronic or mechanical, including photocopy, recording or any information storage and retrieval system, without permission in writing from the publisher.

British Library Cataloguing in Publication Data
A catalogue record for this book is available from the British Library

002-5532 / Printed in the United Kingdom / 3080

ISBN: 978 086388 733 8

Acknowledgements

The author would like to thank:

Heather Daulphin, Pastoral Deputy of Hampstead School – whose creative thinking brought Counselling and the Emotional Literacy Course to Hampstead.

Athy Demetriades (Behavioural Unit Manager until leaving for promotion in 2003) and Glen Stevens, Lead Mentor who became the other thirds of my Emotional Literacy adopted Set (for group working) and with whom it was a real fun adventure to explore the principles and applications of Emotional Literacy – not least in making a film together.

Other members of the Emotional Literacy course: Tim Bown, Lemah Bonnick, Robyn Gardner, Mark Mayne, Liz Scott, Leona Stephenson and Carol Symons.

I would also like to thank Michael Hawkins for agreeing to help me deliver the Peer Buddying course at Hampstead School. Also Hampstead School for financing the Emotional Literacy course and embracing continued development and integration of Emotional Literacy/Intelligence into the school.

Elizabeth Morris – whose course, delivery and continued support are brilliant, together with her Publishing Manager Rachel Carter without whose unstinting help I would not have known how to present this book.

Brief Introduction

In this guide to setting up high quality provision to meet the emotional needs of pupils through a counselling service and peer mentoring programme Emma has achieved the impossible. She has simultaneously provided the reader with a practical blue-print so that they can do the same, or similar, in their school or setting and also given them a very readable, engaging story of the process at Hampstead School.

The development of the counselling service has been a project very dear to Emma's heart – as I know because I am her friend. The rapid increase in take-up of this service amongst the pupils is a tribute to her exemplary work and tireless quest for the best possible support for the young people in the school. What was most heart-warming about the project was that the idea and desire for a peer mentoring programme came from the students themselves. This was made even more exciting when the group who chose to become mentors committed themselves so thoroughly to a demanding programme of training.

I have no doubt that these young people will benefit greatly from embracing this new role in the school and that it will stand them in good stead for the rest of their personal and professional lives. I also have no doubt that they will provide a high standard of support for their peers. The programme required a high level of competence to be achieved and Emma was rigorous and careful in the attention paid to making sure the participants really understood the extents and limits of their role.

Peer mentoring and the provision of a professional counselling service are excellent processes for supporting the social and emotional development of young people in schools. There is no longer a debate about whether emotional literacy development aids academic achievement and supports behaviour and attendance policies. However, increasingly, in my work visiting and consulting in schools throughout the UK, I see depressed – but undiagnosed – children. Pupils who are unable to manage their emotional states and who act them out through violence and the students who remain shadowy and elusive, whilst never achieving anything like their potential because emotional issues block them. These are the pupils that keep us awake at night.

What can we do to support them and, hopefully, transform their experience of life? They need more; they need the support that more focused and specific attention can give them. They need it not just because it would help them be better learners but because it will help them have better lives. I cannot recommend the provision of counselling services and peer support programmes highly enough. This book will give you a short cut to providing an essential service for all those students that you worry about when you go home! I am so pleased that Emma whole heartedly and generously took the opportunity to extend her talents, turn 'author' and write this book.

I hope you use this programme, I recommend it strongly. Even more importantly, I hope your students enjoy and benefit from it too.

Elizabeth Morris
Principal, School of Emotional Literacy, December 2003.

Authors Introduction

In 1985, whilst running a Sixth Form Centre, which developed out of the growth of its parent Comprehensive, I started training as a Counsellor. In 1987 I left the Sixth Form work partly to have more time for that training. Later, to help finance that on-going training I took up part-time teaching in another large comprehensive. In 1996/7 I remember the school's first OFSTED inspection and recall saying to the Head: "A number of staff seem so stressed they could do with help". "So come up with a plan!" was the response - a typical response from a Head whose expertise included the capacity to invite deep involvement from her staff. I was aware that I was part of an Emotionally Literate organisation.

Early in 1999, when I was preparing to extend my counselling work, the Pastoral Deputy at the school came to me and spoke about possible counselling in-house at the school. In the second half of that school year I began offering counselling on two half days per week in one of the school's attic rooms – already set out for one-to-one sessions for visiting counsellors/therapists from a neighbouring psychotherapy clinic – financed by a new initiative: Excellence-in-Cities. Within very few weeks I was told that the initiative was to be the object of a mini OFSTED inspection. It was at this point that my first deliberate piece of Networking took place. I met with the newly appointed Lead Mentor, occupant of another of the school's attics some 100+ stairs away!

Looking back I can now see that it was this piece of networking that led to the Lead Mentor and me to see the need for, and eventually to achieve, a higher profile for Counselling and Mentoring in the school. We are now comfortably established in a discrete building – a totally dedicated area for the Inclusion team, of which we are now a part.

Co-incident with my seeking to work full time in counselling was my contact with a therapist friend, Elizabeth Morris, questioning her as to where her latest research was taking her. One response of Elizabeth was to send me details of two courses, which she had just designed – Certificate and Diploma courses in Emotional Literacy Development. I rather fancied this new learning opportunity and asked my colleague, the Pastoral Deputy, if she would join me in a monthly visit to Bristol University.

To draw this introduction to a conclusion, conversations between the Deputy and Elizabeth Morris led to Elizabeth designing a version of her course to be delivered for a dozen staff at the school, still accredited by Bristol University. For this course I had to present a number of assignments, including a work-related project. As a student of the course I see that work as a logical extension of my development of counselling work at the school. No career is "alive" if it does not involve change. No client (in this case the school) is well served if its employee's work is not held up to that of others in the field and Best Practice followed. It is my belief that counselling will be more effectively targeted at the most appropriate student needs and most successfully followed up where the role of Counselling in the school is more widely understood by staff, parents and students. An umbrella for this was the Emotional Literacy course; my part was to be proactive in testing the efficacy of my belief. The tools I chose were further Networking and a preliminary examination of Peer Buddying central to my hypothesis.

Schools are organic institutions and both endogenous and exogenous shocks to the system make constant revision of ideas necessary. Such revision was necessary during the writing of my original project and is necessary again at this time of writing.

I revised my tools for the project in swapping the setting up of a Drop-In service in favour of extended Networking. The imperative behind this change was the size of the counselling Waiting List, although both staff and students had enquired about the possibility of a Drop-In service. Holding space open for enquiries and crises seemed inappropriate in the shadow of the Waiting List.

What I am presenting here is a revised version of my work for the Emotional Literacy course project-launch, together with the earlier setting up of the Counselling Service in the school and subsequent developments from that basic provision as logical extensions of that work.

Preface to the Second Edition

In the delivery of the Peer Buddying Course to one cohort, the unanimous response of the group in the closing session was: "Please can we have more training?" A great piece of synchronicity was that the colleague who agreed to help me deliver the course to this particular group was the school's Youth Worker, who said: "As it happens, I have some money in my Residentials' Budget". The outcome was a residential weekend immediately following the Year 12 examinations – students today are faced by examinations almost every single year of their secondary schooling.

We designed the weekend so that each further counselling session was preceded / followed by a physical exercise. The physical exercises chosen by Leila the School Youth Worker, were a two hour midnight hike involving map-reading (we did have an expert with us); a moderately demanding assault course; an archery session; an evening of ice-skating and a wind-surfing session. Although it was made very clear there was a choice, all the trainees took part in all of the activities.

The counselling training was mostly practise sessions. We began with a showing of the Gloria Tape – the video recording entitles: "Three approaches to Psychotherapy". I used it to show the students how the founder of Person Centred therapy worked, and showed only the session of Carl Rogers, as I had not introduced the approaches of the other therapists. We then had a discussion to remind us of the Six Core Conditions which were introduced to them in our training modules.

The impact of training and the video were soon demonstrated. At first we gave a number of slots for the students to practice with one another. To finish – indeed the last practice session of the weekend – we asked them to counsel the staff. I was wonderfully impressed by the young man who found himself facing me, accompanied by two of his peers as observers, and who held strongly to his listening role and the Core Conditions. I felt really "held" by that experience.

So what was the outcome of that extension to the course? It demonstrated a significant development of their interpersonal skills – the group became very supportive of its individual members, ready to take on the challenge of Peer Buddying. For the school it proved to be much more effective group than more modestly trained students and, therefore, we determined to include such weekends in subsequent Peer Buddy training. In a very real sense the training cannot be too long and further input via continuing supervision of the Peer Buddies is an integral part of such training.

In just the same way that we found the group building exercise to be helpful at the Residential Weekend and beyond, so too we have extended the idea to physical activity mixed in with the more formal training undertaken. This has proved particularly more helpful where the group is larger. The optimum group size for us is 10/12. The biggest group we have accepted is 15. In the larger groups, gaining trust takes longer and physical activities can speed that process. It has proven especially helpful to work with a trained Youth Worker who has a battery of bonding exercises at her finger tips.

The Peer Buddying programme that I outlined in the first edition of this book has become an established part of the Post-16 Centre's involvement of the students in Community Work. As a way of making the scheme even more integrated into the working of the school we have added a further module to the course in which we involve members of Senior Management of the school; in our circumstance that currently happens to be the Senior Deputy and the Deputy who is the school's Child Protection Officer. They meet the Peer Buddies upon completion of the course. The Senior Deputy invites the Buddies to explain to her what they have learned. She invites comment under the following headings:

1. What skills and knowledge have you gained?
2. What are the key issues for clients?
3. What are the challenges and obstacles for you as a Buddy?
4. What benefits do you gain as a person?

The Deputy who is the Child Protection Officer for the school then outlines what her work in the capacity involves and the need for Buddies to appreciate that not only will complex issues demand referral on to the school's counsellor, but that some issues will demand the attention of the CPO. This, of course, could be via the counsellor or, in their absence (most school counsellors are part-time), directly to the CPO.

Yet a further modification that we have put into effect is the spreading of the material over a greater number of modules where timetabling makes the use of a full afternoon difficult. Our first delivery of the course was over 8 full afternoons. Subsequently we have worked for 12 twilight sessions to surmount timetable difficulties. We have also found it helpful to provide detailed information for the school in the form of leaflets and displays – so that students and staff can become acquainted with who the Peer Buddies are and what they offer to the school. This, of course, is made so much easier with digital cameras that permit downloading directly onto illustrative material.

The additional module material and the documentation for the weekend are added as an appendix to the Peer Buddying Pack, after page 76. The Emotionally Literate Goodbye (an invitation for course members to award each other a brief "positive stroke" inside an outline of the course member's hand) and the award of Certificates is now held over until the Debriefing and Evaluation session of the Residential Weekend.

Preparation for the Programme

Counsellors in schools ideally have an intimate working knowledge of schools – an ex-teacher for instance. If they have no such background then learning about the pressures on the classroom teacher and the multi-tasking of Senior Management would be a useful precursor to working as a school counsellor. Additionally, meeting with such groups as Year Heads, other Support Staff and ultimately with the whole staff is imperative. It is important for staff to air what their expectations are. It is important that the counsellor makes it clear what can be delivered. The counsellor will find flexibility especially appropriate in a school setting. Children do not have adult knowledge; they have little or no economic power; choice for them is very limited; life skills are rudimentary. Precious adherance to boundaries could be damaging.

Management structure and initiatives available to a school will significantly influence the successful integration of a Counselling Service in the school structure. Where there is a high level of Emotional Literacy in the school structure, notably where the staff are themselves either conversant with the principles of Emotional Literacy or where they have put in place programmes to aid Mentoring, Behavioural Issues and Social Skills, then referrals are likely to result in counselling waiting lists rather than students being expected to "pull their socks up and get on with it".

There will always be the thorny issue of Time-Limited counselling versus Open-Ended counselling. My experience has been to allow the decision to be determined student by student. The majority of young people may find that Time-Limited counselling is too rigid a structure, too much, for instance, like exam schedules.

Conversance with Emotional Literacy is a less necessary precursor to the successful integration of a counselling service into school life than the openness of staff to Emotional Literacy learning.

Thought out environmental provision is important at the outset. A designated room; a place that is quiet; a site that is fairly discreetly situated; a room that is appropriately furnished. An ad hoc arrangement of a space will not do. Neither student nor counsellor will be able to build their self-esteem without the school honouring its declared need by offering a quiet place, free from classroom symbols, with comfortable, similar chairs, with a clock that permits both client and counsellor to monitor their use of time. Other important tools include a tape player (perhaps recorder also), games, paper and other drawing/colouring materials. In a school setting you may find that recording sessions is not wanted by the school. You may wish to question its use yourself as well. A phone that has a silent message facility is helpful – connected both to staff and the outside world.

The In-House Counsellor can oil the wheels of integration by Networking with staff: informally in the staff-room and after school; formally by joining meetings, being available for consultation; by contributing more widely to the Emotional Literacy of the school. One possible means is by drafting appropriate policy documents – or serving on an appropriate committee – where this permits the maintenance of necessary boundaries. Another avenue is to investigate the possibility of working with other staff in directly promoting enhanced levels of Emotional Literacy. Yet another possibility is for hands-on input from students in a Peer Buddying Scheme. I hold back from the title of Peer Counselling – the profession has been lax enough in permitting woolly edges to who is and who is not a "counsellor".

4 The Programme

Three particular stages can include:

1. Setting up a Counselling Service.

2. Moving the broader principles surrounding Counselling into the wider school context. This might include further networking with staff and other institutions. It might also be becoming more involved with the "culture" of the school, e.g. policy drafting, courses to raise emotional awareness.

3. Involving the students: a Peer Buddying Scheme.

1. Setting up a Counselling Service

The rationale behind my work has been to achieve a greater awareness amongst staff and students of the part played in education by Emotional Literacy and thereby to achieve happier, more fulfilled lives for staff and students. The consolidation that I set out to achieve (of the role of counselling in the school) began, of course, at the point where I accepted the post of in-house Counsellor. That consolidation, I believe, started with clear documentation for use in the counselling work. Pro Formas of these documents were shared for discussion: some for confidential files ONLY; some to keep track of student referrals and attendance. Thus began my networking. A dedicated Counselling Room with the appropriate facilities earlier referred to is vital and the more effective when seen as part of an inclusion suite/area.

My hypothesis for further consolidation was that more networking and the development of further services like drafting a Bereavement Policy and Peer Buddying would further raise the profile of Counselling in the school. That networking involves talking with groups of staff about what is Counselling and what are its limitations and what further developments can there be – a suitable subject for an INSET day.

The documents with which to begin those discussions and later to use in counselling might include:

a. A notice for posting in Year Rooms about what is counselling and how an appointment may be arranged. A school that is not familiar with what counselling is may need visible reassurance that it is a "normal" part of the school's many services.

b. A notice for posting in the Year Rooms about when Counselling takes place, so that both staff and students can see that it fits in with the school timetable and may also take place after school – a possibility for some students, usually the more senior ones, especially in the winter months with early darkness. Early thinking led me to offer 40 minute sessions but this left uncomfortable gaps for students and a mismatch with the school's timetable. It also proved to be the case that most secondary school students are well able to handle the "normal" 50 minute counselling sessions.

c. A note sheet for information to other members of staff which does not relate to a particular student/client. It is hardly a difficult sheet to design but to have such sheets available in a filing cabinet is convenient and as a regularly appearing sheet will so much better capture the attention of a colleague than a hastily scribbled sheet.

d. An appointment card, both to facilitate the Year Head in arranging times and as a reminder for students of their sessions. Better still they enter their appointments in their School Planner. The appointment card can be copied on card, in a reduced size, from the notice referred to in note b and illustrated on page 28.

e. A referral/attendance/feedback form. When students are offered an introductory session they readily accept the difference between a form for attendance which is open to appropriate staff, and a confidential form kept only by and for the Counsellor.

f. A sheet for introductory/assessing information. CONFIDENTIAL

g. A sheet for ongoing sessions with only a client number at its head. CONFIDENTIAL

h. Mindful of the need to record "outcomes" I designed a sheet (Feedback form from Referrer to Counsellor) which proved unhelpful. In its place I keep a record myself, collated from a variety of sources, regarding students with whom I have "closed" or who are "did-not-attend". The form carries names, student number (my own filing number), place on waiting list, brief outcome. CONFIDENTIAL

i. A timetable sheet (usually per half term) for immediate, daily reference and recording.

j. Analysis sheets to record names, form/year, number of sessions attended/not attended. This information permits cost-effectiveness offering to management, levels of attendance, levels of planned versus d.n.a. closure, varying use of the service by different year groups.

k. Other sheets can include tools for use in the counselling sessions. I make use of Transactional Analysis (T.A.) imagery for working with some students, e.g. T.A. Ego States, T.A. Egograms, T.A. Script Matrix. Counsellors with other orientations for their work will have different aids.

2. Moving the broader principles surrounding counselling into the wider school context.

Beyond the networking necessary simply to learn how the school and locality function, there is extended networking that will signal the degree of integration into the school life that a school counsellor should continuously address. Key for me was the coalescing of design and circumstance – the adoption by the school of a course in Emotional Literacy plus the extension of the Excellence-in-Cities programme to being more fully inclusive. From this good fortune and design, myself, the Behavioural Unit Manager and the Lead Mentor chose to become a "Set" (a working sub-group) in the Emotional Literacy course. Design, because we chose to work together, we chose to join the course, we chose to present our course projects together. Circumstance, because we worked in the same designated area of the school, but until this point were a set of three individuals working on discrete tasks. How much the course taught us to appreciate one another and our JOINT work. It became fun to work together and it bought new outcomes. I cannot imagine a more useful thing for a school counsellor to do than to initiate the adoption of such a course at their school.

Senior Management are clearly responsible for Policy Documents. The best of management teams will turn to others for assistance from time to time. A counsellor could offer input in areas like Bullying and Death & Bereavement. One of the pieces of work for which I have been asked for input was the latter.

In drafting an outline for consideration there were a number of points for attention, not least that whilst a policy in isolation could be administratively helpful, it would be more truly effective where the policy was an integrated part of an Emotionally Literate "culture". One which arises from where the society presently is, to one which seeks to influence that society.

3. Involving the students: a Peer Buddying Scheme.

The raison d'etre of any school is its students. In the 21st Century, the Emotionally Literate School will see students not only as the object, but in many circumstances, the provider of learning and of change. It is in this context that I see the development of a Counselling Service in a school, as one which invites student participation in the provision – or should I say invites participation in the "formal" provision. Many students, without any training, are sympathetic listeners and supportive friends, there is no "them and us" experienced by the confiders; then why not tap that resource?

A useful place to start would be a draft of a Peer Buddying scheme to be discussed with Senior Management. I spent time with two school Deputies and was able thus to address issues like willingness and capacity to make space available; fitting in with school programmes; embracing the co-operation of other staff; possible consultation/training for the Counsellor; deciding on which students would be invited to take part in a pilot project; looking at examples of existing schemes.

There are good schemes already in existence. A little research in your area could well offer the possibility of visiting a school which has a Peer Buddying scheme. There are also good training programmes and I can certainly recommend the ACER course, under the tutorship of Pauline Maskell.

In the accompanying Peer Buddying training material there is a general order, but I have in my mind two particular thoughts, the programme of training needs to be fun, whilst the object of the exercise is the development of the trainee and subsequently the client. The programme will be like most Counselling training, there are materials, concepts and methodology to be covered, but the order of delivery should be participant driven. A preliminary order will be planned.

1. The pack of material which start with the idea common to all humanistic approaches that "You are important." A fictional representation of this can leave an image to remain with the Buddy throughout their work and "visible" through that work to the client.

2. Following logically from this could be a scenario where the Buddy is challenged with "So which students 'need' counselling?" A sentence which would bring as many choices as there are bodies in the picture – the glum face may be no more truly indicative of say inner conflict, than the self-assured body posture of another character illustrated.

3. There are a number of TA (Transactional Analysis) illustrations that appeal to teenagers. I use them in my Counselling Practice. I have in my mind especially:

    - The Egogram
    - An illustration of the Child ego-state sitting next to the Adult ego-state
    - A Script Matrix

4. A useful early idea to introduce is self-awareness. A group exercise in this can be scary and wonderfully releasing. It is most important to monitor how students handle vulnerability. I tried the format headed "Feedback from Referrer to Counsellor." When I designed this form I was mindful of the jargon and demands of OFSTED. However, the form failed to bring the response in writing. Year Heads, very pressured members of staff, preferred to give me verbal feedback. It was thus that I designed the form: "Counselling (Student List)" to include that oral feedback as well as other useful information like Waiting List numbers.

5. Following on and continuing during the course, a personal (PRIVATE) diary of feelings can be encouraged. For those unused to charting their feelings, prepared pages can be helpful and more likely to result in a fairly continuous diary. Failure to complete may be a valuable point for discussion. Making many copies of this could be helpful as during the training course it might be hoped that students complete one after each training session. In this way it is not only a constant reminder about awareness during sessions, it is also a way of alerting any changes that they may bring about.

6. The appointment card could be made by miniaturising the sheet "Counselling at School" and on that text could be added a 6th note looking thus;
      6. Time and date of appointment………………………………..

7. That the training takes a group format introduces the student to the idea that whilst Buddies see the Client alone, the Buddy is always part of a network. It is useful to learn at an early stage that there are others there for the Buddy and/or Client. Continuing supervision will always be a requirement of any such scheme. What, therefore, will be helpful for a group to know about itself?

8. What makes a "good" listener? What are the qualities of a good listener? The two sheets in the pack that encourage students to think around these questions are:

   a) A chart with spaces for students to complete in groups or individually.
   b) A list of suggestions to follow (a) for the entire group to discuss together with their own ideas.

In the Plan/Outline on page 53/54 each session is shown to begin with Group Process. I have found it to be wonderfully rewarding to watch students taking increasing, tho' measured, risks as the programme progresses in the Peer Buddy training. It is, of course, important to remind them to monitor how much they share and what is appropriate not to share in this forum.

9. The group members will have their own ideas about what it is to be a member of a group – or to be excluded from a group. It is useful for the members to be aware in training that they are a resource – they have skills.

10. In the Peer Buddying Pack of material some sheets should be produced only for the trainer – thus all those not listed here are appropriate for the Peer Buddies.

- There could be exercises for developing listening skills (a group whisper) and body awareness skills (preparation for a visualisation exercise and for miming a task). In a Group Whisper the trainer takes a student out of the room and tells them a brief but complex story. Each student then takes it in turn to tell another student out of the room until the last student returns and to the group recounts the story. If you prewrite your piece you will discover, when reading it subsequent to the final student recounting it, how well we do or do not listen.
- In a miming with the same format of miming to a student and them taking it in turns to do the mime in secret, until the last student recounts what they believe they saw when repeating it to the group. I remember Pauline Maskell (see Bibliography) had the wonderful demonstration of washing an elephant. Indeed both the above exercises are most effective if of very "way out" subjects. They are one of many vehicles for introducing fun.
- A register (necessary for all school activities and for awarding a closing certificate).
- In the students' pack of materials should be a Self Awareness Diary sheet. As well as Group Process this sheet relates to number 4 of this list. In addition the trainer should have a set of sheets for the whole group. It will make useful material for the final interview with individual students at the end of the course.
- An illustration of the Drama and Beneficial Triangles may be of use if the group show a capacity and wish to take theory further.

11. Questionnaires – The questionnaires are graduated to reflect the progress of the course and useful tools to encourage the trainees to realise that they had valuable ideas before they began the course that might be brought into awareness. The first of these questionnaires would be most appropriate at the outset of the course; the second at the end. To remove any anxiety it is important to point out that only the individual student will see their sheets (they keep them). They are useful not only as written above, but also to offer material for discussion.

This is not an Academic Study. It is a working document, which sets out procedures and pro-formas, which I have found helpful. The brief text is a statement of how I arrived at this point in my work. The documents are a photocopiable resource which may stand as they are, or be modified to fit a different institutional setting.

That I put this together came from the Action Plan which I chose to be my tangible result of joining the course of The School of Emotional Literacy. It is true that I had already set up a Counselling Service at Hampstead School and that I, therefore, had developed a set of working documents. The course reinforced my wish to extend this introduction of Counselling to a more comprehensive understanding and practice of Emotional Literacy for the broader community of which my service is just a part.

The whole group of students were invigorated by the course and the consequences have been notable and are on-going. As I write this, the Pastoral Deputy is at a National Conference, outlining the school's journey – both achieved and planned.

The Peer Buddying course is the most clear outcome from my own wish more deeply to integrate my work into the school. It is one of those projects, which covers huge institutional and personal rewards. The designing of the course is fascinating, selling the idea to the students is absorbing and you may well find yourself, if setting up such a project, having to find creative ways to reduce numbers for a training group – ideally to, say 12.

Teaching to the course is immensely rewarding. To discover the significant depths of understanding and empathy in the trainees and their capacity to take risks, but not to do so carelessly. This last is most important to emphasise throughout the course.

It is a nice point as to how long the course should last – for me it is 8 bi-weekly sessions (to fit both a timetable running across 2 weeks and also to allow time for students fully to digest their experience). It is very tempting to add to the material and to extend the course. I would recommend not. First, it is important to remember this is a Peer Buddying course not a full Counselling course! Second, it is important not to overload the particular age group targeted – in my case 16/17 years old. Third, on an entirely pragmatic issue, the students need to get down to working with a target group.

That it could be rewarding to take the course further can be compensated for by involving the trainees to go further for themselves – to offer them a Bibliography.

PHOTOCOPIABLE MATERIALS

Pages 22-29, 43-56, 60 and 60-88 are set out to be photocopied or scanned, or modified and photocopied. They form the substance of this working document, the objective of which is to assist counsellors in a setting like a school to have immediate ideas that integrate counselling into the raising of emotional literacy levels and to tap resources that lie latent in the organisation.

Part 1 - Setting up a Counselling Service

You may find it helpful to follow the six steps below.

Step 1: Get to know the school and staff – NETWORKING INTERNALLY

Step 2: PREPARE THE ROOM appropriately for your work, a lockable filing cabinet, two easy chairs, desk to one side, resources like drawing materials, buttons, games, music equipment……….

Step 3: HAVE DOCUMENTS READY – make enough copies for at least one month's sessions – a whole term's copying would leave you feeling prepared (pages 22-29)

Step 4: Make sure you have SUPERVISION in place and ideally paid for by the school.

Step 5: Involve yourself in STAFF/SCHOOL DEVELOPMENT so that you may have the context for suggesting policy ideas, staff insets……

Step 6: Research for yourself local school or national TRAINING DAYS for ideas like PEER BUDDYING……

Note from School Counseller

Counselling Room Tel…………………………....
Mobile ……………..………………………..
To:……………………………………………..
From:………………………………………….
Date:………………………………………….
Message:………………………………………………………………………………
………………………………………………………………………………………..
………………………………………………………………………………………..
Cc:……………………………………………………………………………………..

Counselling at ....

1. Counselling is available at .... There are sessions (of about 50 minutes) available on:
.... between .... and ....
.... between .... and ....

2. Referrals to the counsellor can be made through your Year Head. You may also speak directly with the counsellor, Miss/Mrs/Mr *****.

3. Counselling is entirely CONFIDENTIAL (with exceptions such as life-threatening circumstances) and requests for counselling and a discussion about how counselling may help will remain equally confidential.

4. Counselling is about maximising your own potential; about understanding why you feel, think and behave as you do and about exploring strategies to help to change those feelings, that thinking and behaviour.

5. Whilst you often have wonderful friends, parents and teachers with whom you can speak, there are some issues that seem so personal, to turn to a person whom you only see as a counsellor may offer a greater sense of guaranteed privacy. It may also be helpful to realise that for a whole session(s) you give yourself time to unburden, to explore, to be heard – in the school's Counselling Room.

Referral/Feedback

Student Name .... Form ....

Referred by ....

Placed on Waiting List: date...

Did/did not attend session at ....

Date of next session ....

End of counselling: Closure planned/did not attend ....

Other information that may be communicated ....

....

....

....

cc   CPO
           Line Manager
           Year Head
           Also ....

.... Counsellor

Feedback from Referrer to Counsellor

Please would you use the following Feedback form so that we may monitor the effectiveness of counselling sessions.

DEPUTY HEAD/YEAR HEAD

STUDENT REFERRED……………………………….. FORM…………….

1. Following the student attending counselling will you comment upon changes in:

(a) Attendance………………………………………………………………………

………………………………………………………………………………………

(b) Behaviour ………………………………………………………………………

………………………………………………………………………………………

(c) Participation ……………………………………………………………………

………………………………………………………………………………………

(d) Achievement …………………………………………………………………

………………………………………………………………………………………

or

2. Are there identifiable reasons why ……………………………… chose not to attend counselling sessions? ………………………………………………………

Client Assessment Sheet

Name:..

Male/Female:...............................

Age:................. School Year:.......................Form:..........................

Address:...

....

Referred by:..

Parental Consent:..

Family/Place in family:..

....

Important others:...

Religion:...

Medical History:...

....

Earlier Therapy/counselling:...

Date and Time:...

Client Story:..

....

....

....

Client Pro Forma

Client no………….. Date and time:………………………………………………..

Recording Yes/No…………………..

Appearance………………………………………………………………………………..

New issue/continuation………………………………………………………………….

………………………………………………………………………………………………..

Feelings: Client……………………………………………………………………………

………………………………………………………………………………………………..

    Counsellor……………………………………………………………………

………………………………………………………………………………………………..

Process……………………………………………………………………………………..

………………………………………………………………………………………………..

………………………………………………………………………………………………..

Content……………………………………………………………………………………..

………………………………………………………………………………………………..

………………………………………………………………………………………………..

Closure……………………………………………………………………………………..

………………………………………………………………………………………………..

………………………………………………………………………………………………..

Next session……………………………………………………………………………….

Counselling 20__ - 20__

Wednesday							Thursday						
8.50 – 9.40							8.50 – 9.40						
9.50 – 10.40							9.50 – 10.40						
11.10 – 12.00							11.10 – 12.00						
12.10 – 13.00							12.10 – 13.00						
14.20 – 15.10							14.20 – 15.10						
15.20 – 16.10							15.20 – 16.10						

Counselling (Student List)

Waiting List No.	Student Name	Form	No. of sessions offered	Referred by	Student No. in records	Closure planned/ D.N.A	Feedback

Egogram

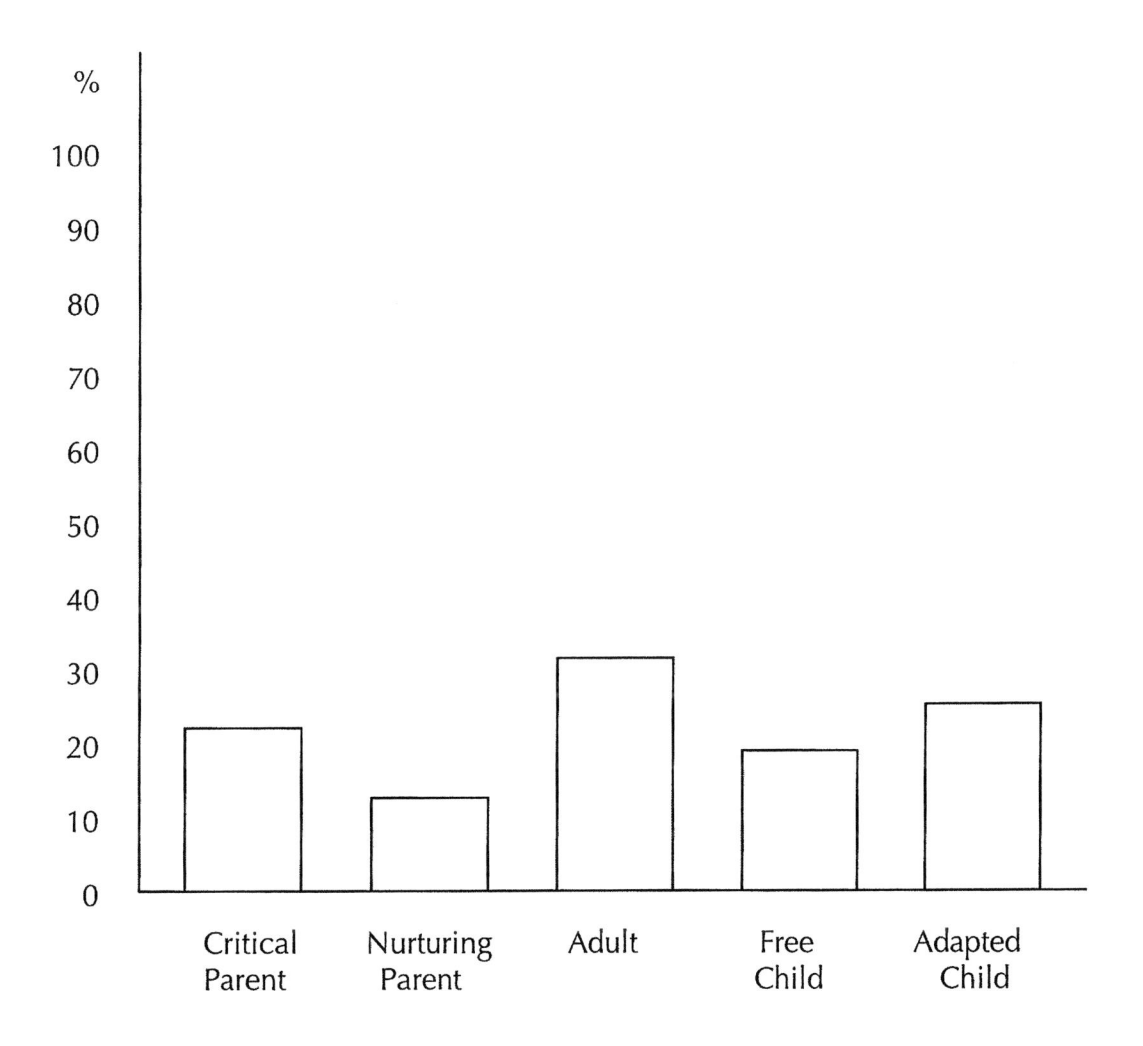

	Critical Parent	Nurturing Parent	Adult	Free Child	Adapted Child
%	~22	~13	~32	~20	~26

Taken from work of Jack Dusay

Script Matrix

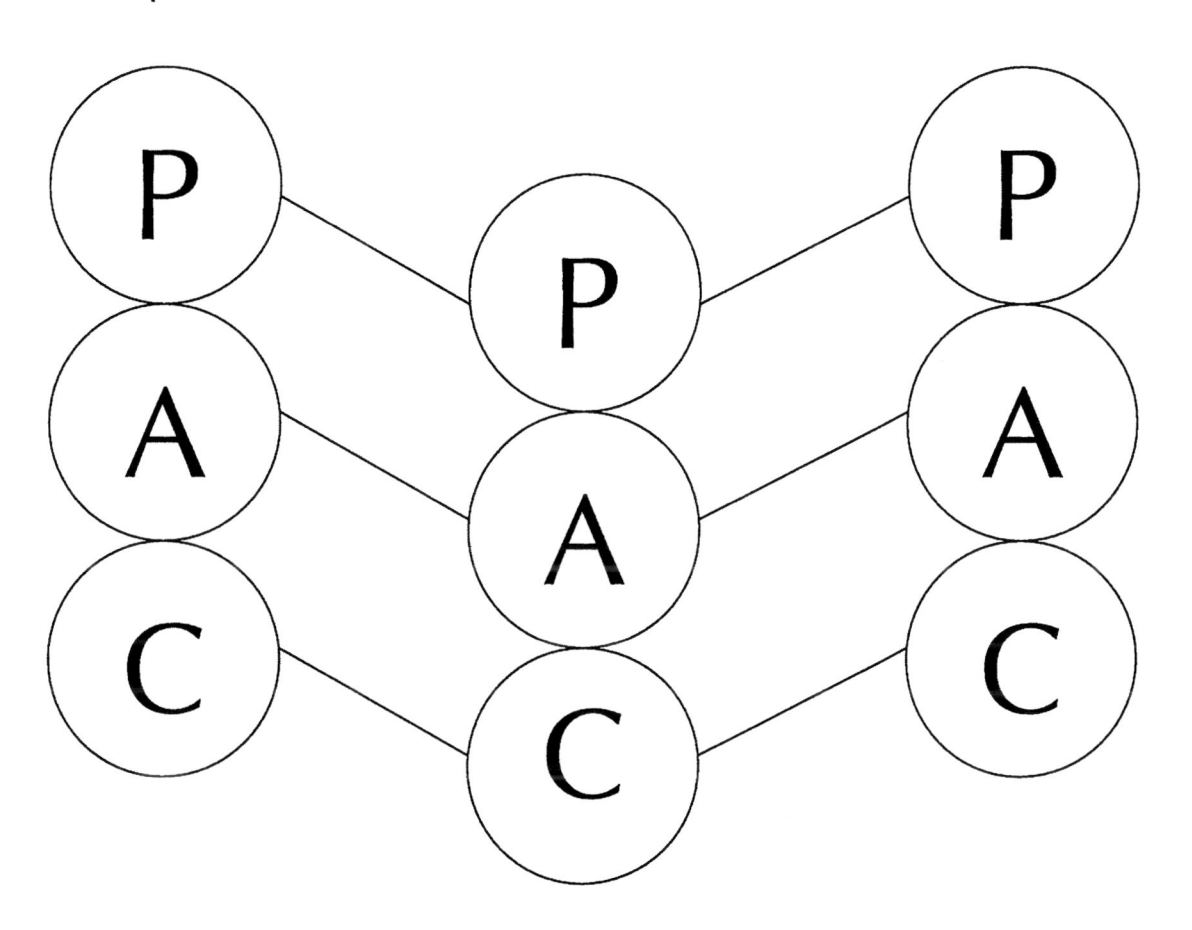

Taken from work of Claude Steiner

Part 2 - The Wider School Context

This section contains areas of the Counsellor's work when moving into the whole school policy area.

In this section I have included my notes for thinking on Confidentiality and a Death and Bereavement Policy. They are partly the consequence of my own networking within the school and partly a means of achieving further integration of the work I do.

A particular issue for counsellors working in schools (or other institutions) is that of Boundaries. There is a real conflict for at least two issues. First, the conflict of what the School and Staff expect of the Counsellor and what the Counsellor may practically and ethically deliver. Second, there is the conflict of wishing to integrate and network whilst remembering that too much contact and too much sharing of information is simply not within the bounds of Confidentiality. The staffroom is a particularly danger-laden zone for loose conversation.

A further issue is that of recognising when the Counselling Service is appropriate for a child and both how available and how open-ended can counselling be. Pastoral staff are particularly sensitive (knowing) to what is appropriate for themselves and where the student may benefit from counselling. It is likely also that the school counsellor will be asked by staff for consultation. I see staff for time-limited work only. This, in part, as I find my time to be filled by students, but also to minimise boundary problems. I sometimes refer staff to local agencies and to other private practitioners. To have names and numbers available is useful.

It is also useful to make links with local psychiatric units or specialist services. Whilst it is important not to pathologise, it is also important to err on the side of caution where pre-psychotic condition seems possible, or where what is presented is outside one's own competence.

Notes on Confidentiality

One important source of information on the matter of confidentiality for those involved with young people is "Working with Young People" produced by the Children's Legal Centre of Essex University. They also produce a number of pamphlets on topics like Bullying and I list some of those in the Bibliography. BACP offer training days on working with young people with input on Confidentiality. Richard Cohen's pamphlet on "School Based Mediation Programmes" had helpful points.

Counsellors will have a heightened sense of what is confidentiality and that it is central to the whole idea of counselling. Nonetheless, at school we are working with Minors and there is a three cornered relationship of Counsellor, Client and Parent/School. The counsellor has a duty to his/her employer as well as The Client and Parent.

---

1. The law does not make a definitive statement of what is Confidentiality, it is generally accepted (and core to the working of a counsellor), that owed to the Client is A DUTY OF CONFIDENCE where agreement has been made that information is confidential.

---

2. At the outset of any professional relationship between the counsellor and the child client, the question must be put to the child as to whether they are willing to inform their parents and to obtain their consent before they proceed beyond a first information session. The counsellor may judge the client to be GILLICK COMPETENT if they believe the child is sufficiently competent to consent for themselves. HOWEVER, A LOCAL AUTHORITY MAY NOT ACCEPT THAT STANCE and require Parental Consent for ALL UNDER 16. Sadly this will mean that a few children will not agree to work with the counsellor beyond the information session and there is little that the counsellor can do in these circumstances.

---

3. By GILLICK COMPETENCE, Case Law refers to the maturity and understanding of the child to the consequences of his/her actions. Whilst there is no age bar imposed, the Legal Centre believe that competence would never be presumed for those under 13.

4. To offer safety to the counsellor and to work to BEST PRACTICE, parental consent should be sought. That a child seeks a preliminary session falls under the DUTY OF CONFIDENCE. Any work beyond this could require parental consent. However, the CONTENT of the counselling IS CONFIDENTIAL with the usual counselling cautions.

5. All counselling has its boundaries and these must be made clear in the ASSESSMENT/INTRODUCTORY session. Concern for a young person's health and well-being MUST over-ride concern for confidentiality.

Notes on Death and Bereavement

Death is the great taboo in a society hooked on the Media Youth Culture, but to our cost as potential bereaved. A school, therefore, requires a PLANNED response that EDUCATES about Death, Rituals and Mourning and provides a SENSITIVE and COMPASSIONATE environment which offers group and individual discussion to loosen the hold of the taboo.

The policy needs to be understood in the context of, as well as being an expression of, EMOTIONAL LITERACY.

This could therefore set such a policy in 3 STAGES:

1. A PRE-PLANNED programme that educates about death, rituals and mourning. This could well be built into a comprehensive, emotionally literate PHSE course. The programme should bear in mind that GRIEF is the emotional response to death, whilst MOURNING is the form/process used to portray that. Hence there will be significant cultural and religious contexts that will vary and also, coincidentally, may offer more comfortable vehicles for education in this area.

2. The PRO-ACTIVE stage that embraces notes C/F below and could well conclude with a memorial service.

3. The RE-ACTIVE stage that provides long-term caring for a bereavement experienced.
- Adolescents experience loss (of childhood) and separation (from parents) in striving for independence and identity that are the very stuff of this growing-up period. Bereavement, from death of a friend or relative, serve to underscore that sense of loss and separation.
- The bereaved's reactions may well bring to their life and classroom, denial, anger, depression, aggression, anti-social behaviour and self-harm, in seeking to gain feelings of control. I remember attending the 2002 North London conference on response to catastrophic events and my awareness of the need not to "pathologise" a client's immediate response. The immediate period may well be too soon for formal Counselling. Just being there will be the first response.
- Thus, the allocated (personal) tutor should keep a watching brief directly and through colleagues for a significant time.
- Formal counselling may be of help later.

Therefore:

A. The school should have a KNOWN TEAM the raison d'etre of which is to minimise disruption and restore a sense of safety to the bereaved.

B. The team could include:
- The Team Leader, say the Head (who could also handle Media);
- A Named Tutor - for the bereaved;
- Representative from teaching and non-teaching staff;
- The Counsellor and School Nurse for team, staff and bereaved as required.

C. The Team Leader needs to be certain of ALL THE FACTS.

D. ALL STAFF should be informed before students are informed and this information should be communicated early.

E. CONFIDENTIALITY must be maintained and therefore any comment beyond the fact of death should be avoided. Any further information is the property of the family to release. It is also their choice as to who might attend the funeral.

F. A school assembly can be used to inform; the CLASSROOM is the place for the expression of feelings and Team members may help the teachers not confident around the issue of death.

Part 3 - Peer Buddying Pack - Involving the Students

Preface for Peer Buddying Trainer	38
At-a-Glance Guide to Peer Buddying Training material	41
Trainer's explanatory page	42
Student Register	43
Student Profile (assessed)	44
Plan/Outline of Training Sessions	45
You are important	47
"What qualities would make a Buddy" bubble for brain-storming	48
What makes a Good Buddy	49
So which students need counselling?"	50
Self-awareness diary sheet	51
Student Profile (self-assessed)	52
What makes a good listener? What are the qualities of a good listener?	53
Qualities of a Good Listener	54
Questionnaire No 1	55
Person Centred Counselling	57
Egogram	58
Script Matrix	59
Should you let a Junior take your classroom decisions?	60
Drama and Beneficial Triangles	61
Group visualisation	62
Feelings Figures	63
Emotional literacy	68
Multiple intelligences	69
Skills analysis	70
Final student questionnaire	71
Peer Counsellors – final session	74
An emotionally literate "goodbye"	87
Peer Buddying Certificate	88

Preface for Peer Buddying Trainer

There are eight suggested sessions listed here – a series of sessions of about 24 hours content with the group members. Like all work in this field, time between training sessions to absorb what has been experienced is important. I would therefore recommend a start in mid September so the term than has time to get started and progressing fortnightly to January or the early Spring Term. In succeeding years additional Buddy groups can be trained – start with a pilot group.

There is a lot more material available and what may suit one course may be less useful for another. Thus, for instance, in the same way as session 4 "Exercise in Recall – a Group Whisper" can, with elaborate delivery by the trainer(s) both be fun and training in listening; so, too can a group "demonstration" be fun and training in watching/observing.

The trainer(s) can assemble from this pack, material for the group members. If each member is offered a folder and copies of the outline of the sessions together with plain sheets, subsequent hand-outs will give them material for succeeding sessions. Going armed with spare copies is always advisable and the diary sheets are best issued in significant quantities. The trainer(s) will determine which sheets are appropriate at the outset of the session and which part way through an exercise.

It is important to encourage sharing of opinion and experience between the group members. It is also important to advise erring on the side of confidentiality of students' own work, until they know what they feel is safe to share, or that they are strong enough to withhold. Thus I would expect the two questionnaires, when completed, to remain confidential to the writer, as with the diary pages. They can be invited to discuss what feels truly safe for them. In this way they can gain greater understanding of Confidentiality and the preparedness, or otherwise, of their peers to let go of information.

The brief introduction to Person Centred Counselling and to Transactional Analysis are meant to be just for that. For the really enquiring student a short reading list may be appropriate. However, the course is for Buddies, it is not a course in Counselling. Nonetheless, a good starting point may be to indicate that the approach(es) is/are essentially Humanistic. The introduction to Person Centred Counselling can be talked about using Carl Rogers' "necessary and sufficient conditions". The introduction to Transactional Analysis can be done via the Egogram on page 58 and the Script Matrix on page 59. The trainer could also refer to the two pictures on page 47 and 53. Other counselling orientations could also offer material, but I believe that Person Centred Counselling and Transactional Analysis are ideal introductory approaches to counselling for such a Buddying course. This is not a full Counsellor training course. For such a brief course emphasis is placed on Process – (what is going on). A list of what the trainer(s) need to start could include:

Refreshments
Timetable of the day and of the course
Flip chart and markers
Paper and pens
Training packs
Some text on Counselling and Emotional Literacy for student perusal
A box of tissues

I have been wonderfully fortunate at Hampstead in having an Emotionally Literate colleague to help me deliver the course! Thus, for example, he has been brave enough to offer himself as a Client with REAL material – to enable the students to observe an actual counselling session. The feedback has been excellent. Indeed, in sharing this with my own Counselling Supervisor, I was able to say that it reminded me of the Peer Supervision I received when I was a student of Counselling Supervision.

In the delivery of the course it is my object, simultaneously to honour the significant capacity that the teenage trainees (in this case) have, whilst at the same time reminding them that this is for Buddying – they will not be Counsellors at this time.

Constantly I am wanting to add to the course material. Equally I am aware that what is here could take much longer than the 24 hours of the course. What is learned is certainly deserving of recognition and for a Certificate of attendance ceremony. When the students are ready to meet clients then THEY must make the decision as to how they should be introduced to them – via assembly, year meeting, in Tutor Groups... and then, ideally, be available some times so that younger students would become familiar with them and brave enough to seek confidential sessions. Then the Buddies need Supervision Sessions.

For this brief course emphasis is placed on Process and Practice.

Process can be scary and it would be well to keep it limited in time – a specific slot – and demonstrated at first by the trainers. Ideally the course needs two trainers: one to permit non-scary demonstrations and the other to offer students a variety of approach and a greater sense of balanced judgement when decisions are made that a student is or is not immediately ready to be a Buddy.

At-a-Glance Guide to Peer Buddying Training Material

You may find it helpful to remind yourself and sometimes the group members of the following 10 significant points.

1. Process is important to this training group, but individual members may not always be ready to share their feelings and thinking in a session(s).
2. The diary sheets may offer a "safer" outlet for such feelings and thoughts and using those sheets is to be regularly encouraged. These are useful to remind students that they do NOT have to share everything.
3. The theory introduced in such a brief course is only a taster and therefore those interested could have their attention drawn to user-friendly material.
4. Whilst students will be invited to choose "Who needs counselling here?" at the outset of the course it can be useful to revisit that idea throughout the course.
5. Notice the similarity or difference between body language and spoken word – at the time.
6. Remember and honour your own value system but accept that the client's value system may differ.
7. Exercises can be fun – all of them will contribute to heightening awareness of the demands of listening and observing.
8. As the group work together they will feel increasingly safe – point out to them that their client(s) can experience the same growth of trust.
9. Point out to students that on-going Supervision will be necessary.
10. Don't leave it to the last session to let the Buddies know that the course outcome maybe that:
    (a) the course stands alone as a valuable piece of learning;
    (b) to go for interview and with the trainers agree they are ready to be available for clients – or not ready to be available.

Peer Buddying Training Material

This is an explanatory page for the trainer. There is a general order to this material but I have in mind two particular thoughts. The programme needs to be fun - the object of the exercise is the development of the Trainee and the Client. The programme will be like most Counselling training: material and concepts to be covered, but the order should be participant driven.

In brief:

1. I would like the "pack" to start with the idea common to Humanistic approaches - that "you are important simply because you exist".
2. There are useful TA illustrations, especially for clients wanting to know, when thinking of 'where does that piece of behaviour/feeling/thinking come from?' For example, I use the Child ego state sitting beside the classroom Adult ego state when asking: 'How were you feeling when you thought/behaved like that?'
3. Material to invite ideas from the trainees are a good starting point for thinking around: "So who do you think needs counselling here?"
4. Some good basic outlines for the trainer to bear in mind when preparing a training group.
5. A useful early idea to introduce is Self-Awareness- a group exercise in this is possible.
6. Following on and continuing during the course a personal (Confidential) diary of feelings can be encouraged.
7. That the training takes a group format introduces the student to the idea that whilst Buddies see the client alone, the Buddy is always part of a network. It is useful to learn at an early stage that there are others there for Buddy and/or Client. Continuing Supervision would always be a requirement of any such scheme as the one proposed.
8. Trainers' assessment of trainees.
9. Exercises include: a Listening exercise; Washing an Elephant - to be used at Appropriate training points. At the end the group need to say their goodbyes at the various courses I have attended, a valuably inclusive exercise is for each student to take an A3 sheet and outline their hand. All the group add positive comments on the owner of that sheet. The students need to be informed of this before the session.
10. Questionnaires: The purpose of questionnaires at points in the course is to heighten self-awareness. The questionnaires are therefore confidential to the filler-in.

Student Register

Name	Date							

Student Profile (Assessed)

Scores 1 (high) – 5 (low) (degrees of involvement)

Name..

Date									
Process									
Break									
Theory									
Practice									
Self-awareness									
Awareness of Others									

Plan/Outline of Training Sessions

Session 1   Introduction : Process and Content – trainers demonstrate Process
- You are important
- What qualities would make a Buddy
- Refreshment break
- Visit to Counselling Room
- Which student "needs" counselling?
- Self-Awareness Diary of feelings

Session 2 Group Process
- Demonstration counselling session
- Refreshment break
- Handout "What makes a good listener?" sheet
- Handout the list of "Qualities of a good listener"
- Discussion
- Peer Buddies' first questionnaire

Session 3 Group Process
- Teaching slot on approaches to counselling, especially Person Centred counselling. See notes on Person Centred Counselling
- Refreshment break
- Other approaches e.g. TA via Egogram and Script Matrix perhaps introduce via picture of two Ego States – Should you let a junior take your classroom decisions?
- Drama and Beneficial Triangles

Session 4 Group Process
- Demonstration counselling session
- Refreshment break
- What skills was the counsellor using in the session? How would you have felt if you had been the listener there?
- Exercise in Recall – a Group Whisper
- Ask for background (mood) music for next session

Session 5 Group Process
- How in touch are you with your own body? Group visualisation. (Bring music in case students forget)
- Refreshment break
- Return to looking at feelings and how safe it is to discuss them
- Look at Alphabet of Emotions

Session 6 Group Process
- Counselling session demonstration and feedback
- Refreshment break
- Emotional Literacy definition and principles (handout)
- Students, in pairs, go off to offer each other a 15 minute counselling session. Return to group to express resultant feelings and thinking.

Session 7 Group Process
- Counselling session for students in different pairs. Return to group to express resultant feelings and thinking
- Refreshment break
- Multiple Intelligences (handout)
- Skills analysis (handout)
- Final Student Questionnaire
- An Emotionally Literate Goodbye (positive comments offered to fellow students)

Session 8 Buddy Interviews with both trainers
- Certificate awarding (this could be a separate ceremony)

You are important

What Qualities Would Make a Buddy

Buddy

What Makes A Good Buddy?

1. Sits quietly

2. Sits comfortably and with relaxed body language

3. Makes sure seat is not in 180 degree line with client so that you can look at client without the client having to look back

4. Quietly voiced in approach

5. Does not interrupt – permits client to finish

6. Does not judge what the other person says or offer opinion not asked for

7. Is prepared to wait and not be afraid of silence

8. Briefly feeds back what they think they've heard

9. Holds on to offering an opportunity for the client to feel heard and accepted – knows this is not a conversation between friends

*** This is in no way a definitive list. A good listener may well have other qualities, too.

"So which student(s) need(s) counselling?"

Self-Awareness Diary Sheet

Day....................... Month .... Year.....................

Tick 3 boxes to indicate which were important to you today

☐ What did I feel?...
Did I openly express that feeling? YES/NO Did others notice? YES/NO

☐ What did my body language say?...
Was it open or closed to others? OPEN/CLOSED

☐ Did I talk to all the group members? YES/NO Do I remember their comments? YES/NO

☐ Was there something that I felt uncomfortable about? YES/NO
....

☐ How do I feel about and deal with silence in the group? ....
....

☐ What change do I want in me? ....
....

☐ What changes have I allowed myself to experience?...........................
....
....

Any comments (on above or other feelings)
....
....
....

Student Profile (Self-Assessed)

Scores 1 (high) – 5 (low)   (degrees of involvement)

Name……………………………………………….

Date									
Process									
Break									
Theory									
Practice									
Self-awareness									
Awareness of Others									

Signed……………………………………

What makes a Good Listener? What are the qualities of a Good Listener?

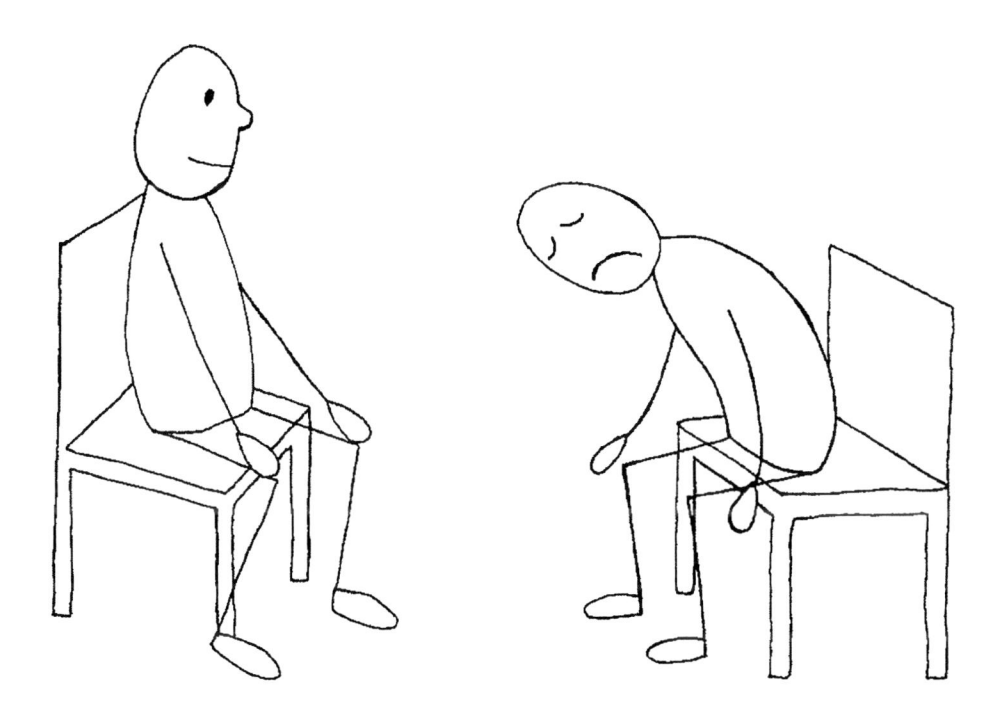

1. ....

2. ....

3. ....

4. ....

5. ....

6. ....

7. ....

8. ....

Qualities of a Good Listener

Non-judgemental/accepting

Empathic

Attach importance to body language

Use feedback and eye contact to demonstrate that attending

Comfortable with the emotions of the client

Aware of own feelings but leave them aside for dealing with elsewhere

Unhurried and patient – with silence, difficulties of speech……

Invite further explanation and exploration

Attend to all content but seek to check main issue(s)

Congruent

Questionnaire No 1

1. What issues are you most aware of as a concern to the students of this school? Put them in order of importance for attention

Homework
Exam grades
Bullying
Street crime
Substance abuse
Loneliness
Friendship
Family relationships
Relationships with teachers
Racism
Sex
Other ………………………………………

2. Where do young people go for help?

Parents
Other adults out of school
Teachers
Counsellors
Other ……………………………………

3. Given your answers to questions 1 and 2.

How well does the school presently cater for the above? ………………………

………………………………………………………………………………………

………………………………………………………………………………………

How could Peer Buddies help?………………………………………………………

………………………………………………………………………………………

………………………………………………………………………………………

What would you expect this course to do to enable you to be more effective and know when to advise the client to take it further?..

....

....

....

Person Centred Counselling

Carl Rogers' necessary and sufficient conditions (from a paper in 1959)

"For therapy to occur it is necessary that these conditions exist:

1. that two persons are in CONTACT;
2. that the first person (the Client) is in a state of INCONGRUENCE, being VULNERABLE or ANXIOUS;
3. that the second person (the Therapist) is CONGRUENT in the relationship;
4. that the therapist is experiencing UNCONDITIONAL POSITIVE REGARD towards the client;
5. that the therapist is experiencing an EMPATHIC understanding of the client's frame of reference;
6. that the client PERCEIVES, at least to a minimal degree, conditions 4 and 5."

These six conditions are well explained in "Person Centred Counselling in Action" by Mearns and Thorne, Sage 1988.

They are brought up to date by Keith Tudor, "The case of the lost conditions" BACP Journal 11/1 (February 2000)

Egogram

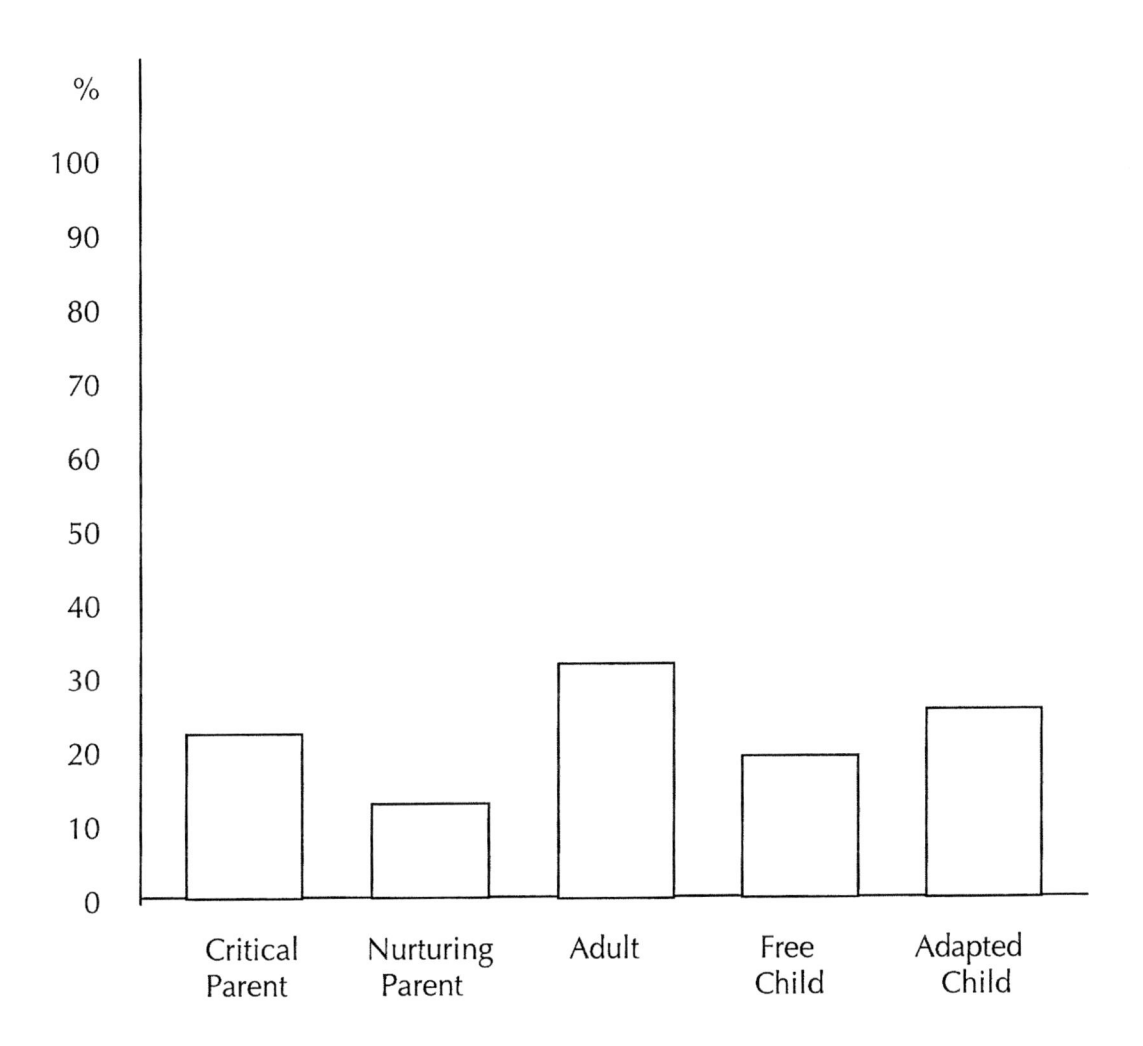

	Critical Parent	Nurturing Parent	Adult	Free Child	Adapted Child
%	~23	~13	~33	~20	~27

Taken from work of Jack Dusay

Script Matrix

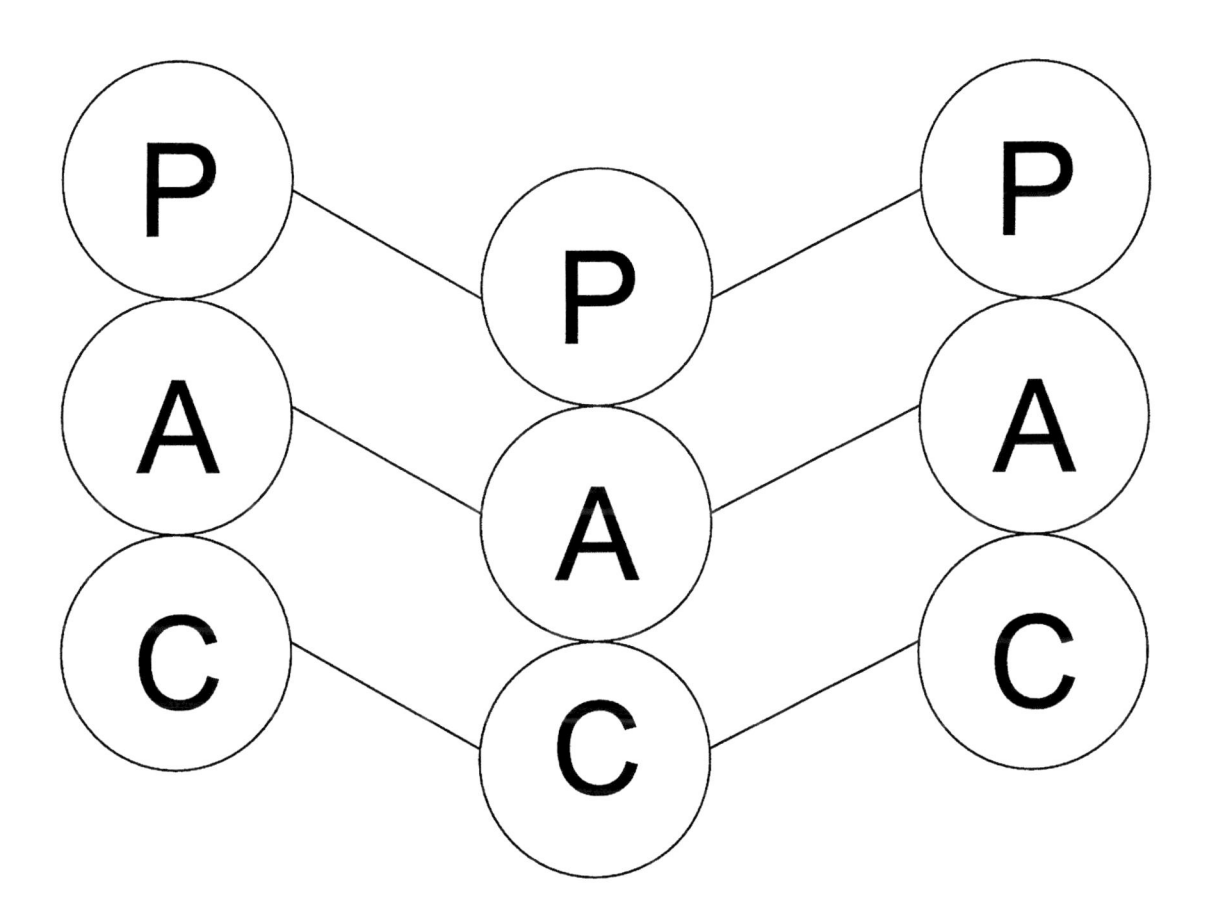

Taken from work of Claude Steiner

Should you let a Junior take your classroom decisions?

Drama Triangle

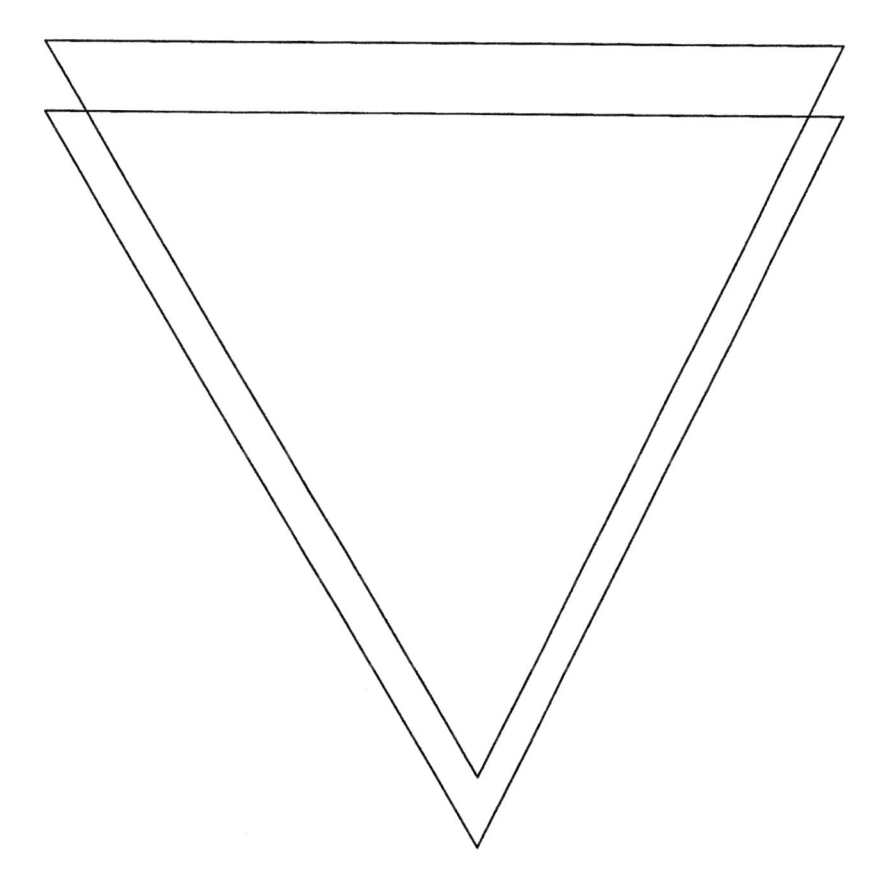

I have drawn this double diagram to illustrate Karpman's Drama Triangle (1968) and extended by the unpublished work of J. Hunt and made accessible by Brigid Proctor – The Beneficial Triangle. It could be helpful for clients to become aware that they may be invited (or invite) another to enter a Drama Triangle and they may be able to save themselves and the other person (s) from the Expected Disappointment by engaging in thinking and behaviour that could lead to the Hoped for Outcome. We can add the labels: Victim/Rescuer/Persecutor and Vulnerable/Responsible/Powerful in the explanation.

Group Visualisation

1. Invite group members to relax in a comfortable chair or on the floor

2. Invite the group members to get in touch with all parts of their body – allowing some moments between each stage:

Wiggle toes; then
Become conscious of calves of their legs; then
Move their attention to their thighs; then
To the abdomen; followed by
Consciousness of their chest through breathing deeply; then
To their arms, hands and then
Their head.

3. Allow the body to relax – accompanied by 'mood' music. Talk the group into a visualisation agreed at the outset. Permit them time to enjoy their visualisation. Bring them out of this process by the getting-in-touch exercise in reverse.

Feelings Figures

Angry

Brave

Content

Curious

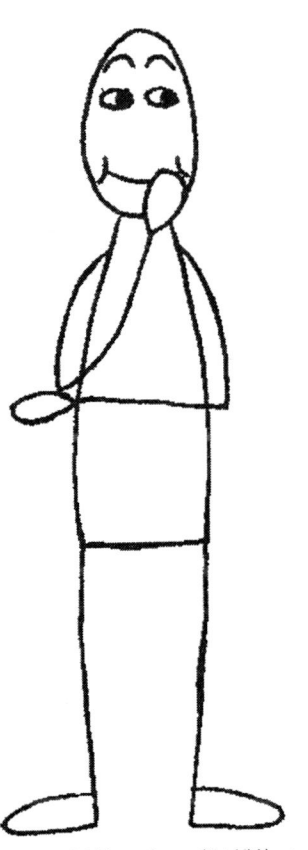

Depressed

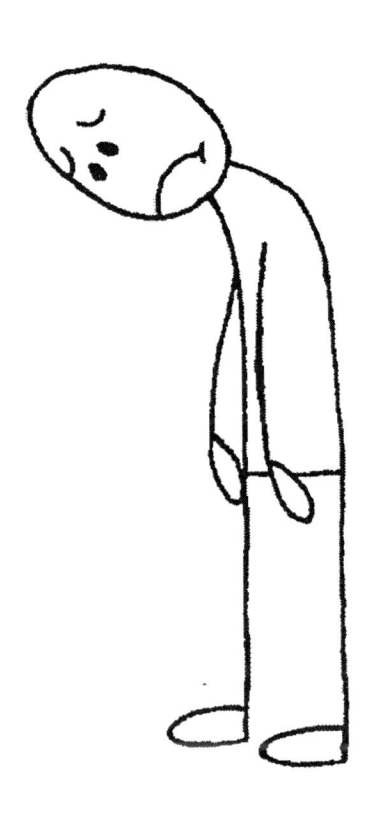

Disgusted

Embarrassed

Happy

Interested

Jealous

Lonely

Loving

Misunderstood

Nervous

Sad

Scared

Shocked **Violent**

Emotional Literacy

Definition: "Recognising, understanding, handling and appropriately expressing emotions in ourselves and other people."

Elizabeth Morris, School of Emotional Literacy

Principles:

1. We are each of us in control of, and responsible for, our actions.

2. No-one else can control our feelings.

3. People are different – in experience, feelings and wants.

4. However you and they are is OK (not necessarily what you <u>DO</u>)

5. Feelings and behaviour are separate. (In the therapy world we work with feelings, behaviours and thinking and invite changes in them)

6. All feelings are justified, acceptable and important

7. Change is possible

8. Physis – all people have a natural tendency towards growth and health

Multiple Intelligences

Definition: "the ability to solve problems or to create products that are valued within one or more cultural setting."

Howard Gardner, 1993

Verbal-Linguistic
Mathematical-Logical
Spatial
Bodily-Kinesthetic
Musical
Interpersonal
Intrapersonal
Naturalist

Skills Analysis

Groups of skills:
1. Self-awareness
2. Self-management
3. Awareness of others
4. Managing others

Individual Skills:
1 (a) Reflection
1 (b) Bodily Awareness
1 (c) Problem Solving
1 (d) Decision Making

2 (a) Heart Smart
2 (b) Anchoring
2 (c) Verbalising feelings
2 (d) Energy Management
2 (e) Mood Management
2 (f) Asking for what want
2 (g) Knowing body signals
2 (h) Goal Setting
2 (i) Anger Management
2 (j) Stress Resilience
2 (k) Self-talk
2 (l) Impulse Control

3 (a) Empathy
3 (b) Body-language – literate/Openness/Tolerance
3 (c) Risk evaluation and trusting regard for others

4 (a) Negotiation
4 (b) Mediation
4 (c) Respectful concentration
4 (d) Apologising and making amends
4 (e) Conflict Handling
4 (f) Giving Feedback
4 (g) Complimenting
4 (h) Tolerance of Differences
4 (i) Resisting pressure – emotional blackmail

Final Student Questionnaire

1. Did I keep a diary of feelings? YES/NO

2. Do I want to express what use that was for me? YES/NO ....

   ....

   ....

3. Do I accept the importance of CONFIDENTIALITY in ALL client – buddy exchanges? YES/NO

4. What would I say to a student, meeting them for the first time as a Buddy, to let them know what I would HAVE to take to my supervisor? ....

   ....

   ....

5A. Looking at the list of good listener qualities which did you find most obvious?

   ....

5B. Looking at the list of good listener qualities which did you find most difficult for you? ....

6. Which training session did you find most interesting? ....

   ....Can you say why? ....

   ....

7. From the person centred counsellors "creed" which do you think is the easiest to follow?

....

....

....

8. Do you think your personal Egogram has changed over the course?
YES/NO

9. Which do you think is your most powerful intelligence? ....

10. Which intelligence do you think would help you most in work as a Buddy?

....

....

11. How comfortable would you feel talking about your individual skills as listed in the skills analysis list?

☐ Very comfortable
☐ Comfortable
☐ Uncomfortable
☐ Very uncomfortable

12. What compliments would I like to offer each member of the group? Write down one of them..

....

....

13. Am I OK sharing that with them? YES/NO..

14. What differences would I have liked in the course?................................

....

....

....

....

Peer Counsellors – final session

1. Skills and knowledge

....
....
....
....
....
....
....
....
....
....

2. Key issues for the clients

....
....
....
....
....
....
....
....
....
....

3. Challenges/obstacles for you as a buddy

Issue	Solution

4. Benefits to you

....
....
....
....
....
....
....
....
....
....

Peer Buddy Programme

Summary papers to illustrate Main Course, follow-up Residential Weekend and Feedback.

Contents

1.	Main course modules (i)	77
2.	Guidelines for Peer Buddies	79
3.	Final interview questions	80
4.	Residential - programme of activities	81
5.	Counselling sessions - at Residential	82
6.	Counselling session analysis	83
7.	Student evaluation form	84
8.	Letter to Parent (s)	85
9.	Information sheet for school of the Peer Buddy resource (ii)	86

Notes

(i) I here include a variant number of modules used by us when timetabling prevents 8 full (3 hour) afternoons.

(ii) These were available in school before a full display was put up, both in the main entrance and in the Year 7 room.

Course Modules

Module 1
Introduction – process and content
Humanistic philosophy – "you are important…."
Confidentiality
Qualities of a Buddy
Personal diary of feelings

Module 2
Group process
Counselling demonstration – session 1
Feedback
What makes a good listener?
Visit to the Counselling Room

Module 3
Group Process
Person Centre approach (i)
PB first questionnaire

Module 4
Group Process
Conditions of Worth questionnaire
Drivers
Person Centred approach (ii)

Module 5
Group Process
Transactional Analysis approach
Two illustrations

Module 6
Group Process
Counselling demonstration – session 2
Feedback
Group "Whisper"

Module 7
Group Process
Visualisation
Alphabet of Emotions
Safety of discussing emotions

Module 8
Group Process
Applications of TA – OK Corrall; Drama Triangle….
Students' counselling practice

Module 9
Group Process
Emotional Literacy
Students' counselling practice

Module 10
Group Process
Multiple Intelligences
Students' counselling practice

Module 11
Group Process
Human Brain
Poem
Students' counselling practice

Module 12
Group Process
Group theory
Final student questionnaire
Hand charts

Peer Buddy certification interviews

Guidelines for Peer Buddies

1. You must meet regularly for SUPERVISION.

2. When you are approached by a student for a private session you must offer CONFIDENTIALITY but inform them that there are issues where you MUST tell someone else – the Counsellor, Year Head or Senior Manager – tell them at the beginning of your work together.

3. The issues for which you will most likely to be competent and not always need to refer on will be about SCHOOL and FRIENDS.

4. Remember that questions should be OPEN questions and not LEADING questions.

5. Remember that you are LISTENING to the client and not having a friendly chat.

6. Keep an eye on the time and try to warn the client when you are nearing the end of the time.

7. You are there to bring choices of thinking, behaving and feeling to the client, NOT ADVICE.

8. Remember what we understand by BOUNDARIES.

9. Offer the client a safe SPACE.

10. If in any doubt take it to your SUPERVISOR, who is also there for you.

Final Interview Questions

1. What is the most useful learning that you think you have achieved through the course?

2. What was the least comfortable incident/piece of learning that you experiences in the course?

3. On a scale of 1-10, in achievement of Emotional Literacy, would you put yourself: (i) at the outset of the course;
    (ii) at the completion of the course?

4. Did you complete any diary sheets during the course?

5. If your answer for 4 was "Yes" did those diary sheets teach you anything? If your answer was "No" why do you think you did not complete any sheets?

6. Do you think you would like to offer help, say, to Year 7 students?

7. If "Yes" to the above question 6, what counselling skill would best serve you?

8. If you "took on" a client when do you think you would say: "this client needs a more qualified listener"?

9. Would you like to take part in more training sessions if they were possible?

10. What did you think about the content of the course?

11. How was the setting?

12. Would you have preferred a different method/order of presenting the course?

13. What would your comments be about the size and make-up of the group?

14. Do you think this introductory course has opened any "doors" for you?

Residential – Programme of Activities

	FRIDAY	SATURDAY	SUNDAY
8.30am – 9.00am	BREAKFAST	BREAKFAST	BREAKFAST
9.30am			
10.00am		Challenge Course & Problem Solving activities	Watersports Windsurfing & Kayaking
10.30am			
11.00am			
11.30am			
12.00pm			
12.30pm			
1.00pm – 2.00pm	LUNCH	LUNCH	LUNCH
2.00pm		Counselling workshop 2	Debriefing session & evaluations
2.30pm			
3.00pm			**Leave**
3.30pm		Archery	
4.00pm			
4.30pm			
5.00pm	Arrive		
5.30pm			
6.00pm – 7.00pm	DINNER	DINNER	DINNER
7.00pm	Counselling workshop 1	Counselling workshop 3	
7.30pm			
8.00pm			
8.30pm		Ice skating Guildford Town Centre	
9.00pm	Night Hike		
9.30pm			
10.00pm			
10.30pm			
11.00pm			

Counselling Sessions – Contents

SESSION ONE: (1.5 hours)

7.30 – 8.00pm	Video: 'Carl Rogers'.
8.00 – 8.10pm	*Short break*
8.10 – 8.20pm	Brief discussion on video: thoughts, feelings and comments.
8.20 – 8.50pm	Counselling sessions: students to practice with other students – one to one.
8.50 – 9.00pm	Discussion and debriefing

SESSION TWO: (2 hours)

2.00 – 2.30pm	Video: "How Not To Do It'.
2.30 – 2.40pm	*Short break*
2.40 – 3.50pm	Counselling sessions: Students to practice with other students – one to one (FILMED SESSION)
3.50 – 4.00pm	Discussion and debriefing

SESSION THREE: (1.5 hours)

7.00 – 8.00pm	Students to counsel staff (mock)
8.00 – 8.10pm	*Short break*
8.10 – 8.30pm	Discussion and debriefing

Counselling Session Analysis

1. How comfortable was the client at the beginning of the session?

   ....

   ....

   ....

2. What did the client say they wanted to talk about?

   ....

   ....

   ....

3. Was that the "real" issue do you think?

   ....

   ....

   ....

4. Did the counsellor show any of the following qualities?
   Empathy
   Congruence
   Unconditional Positive Regard

5. Could you identify if the client demonstrated what was their Ego State (Parent/Adult/Child) at the time of the session?

   ....

   ....

6. What might you have done differently?

   ....

   ....

   ....

Student Evaluation Form

Name (optional):_____ Form:_____

How would you rate the following: ☺   😐   ☹

The accommodation:	[ ]	[ ]	[ ]
The food:	[ ]	[ ]	[ ]
The Staff:	[ ]	[ ]	[ ]
The activities:	[ ]	[ ]	[ ]
The counselling sessions:	[ ]	[ ]	[ ]
School staff:	[ ]	[ ]	[ ]
The atmosphere:	[ ]	[ ]	[ ]
The residential as a whole:	[ ]	[ ]	[ ]

What skills/knowledge have you gained from this weekend?

_____

_____

How can these skills be applied to your future as a 'peer buddy'?

_____

_____

Did you experience any difficulties over the course of the weekend?

_____

_____

If so, how did you deal with them?

_____

_____

How can we further support you in becoming a successful 'peer buddy'?

_____

_____

To what extent has this residential met your expectations? ☺ [ ] 😐 [ ] ☹ [ ]

Letter to Parent(s)

Dear Parent (s)

Now that.. has completed our course in Peer Buddying, and where necessary has caught up with modules missed, we have issued certificates of attendance.

Although.. is a member of the Post-16 Centre at Hampstead, we feel it is appropriate to ask your permission for her/him to undertake Buddying at the school. It is a significant role to take on, but also a great potential contribution to the well-being of younger students at the school. All Buddies will be asked to attend supervision should they engage in any of this work to ensure the best care of Client and Buddy. The Buddies are already aware that there will be issues beyond their competence and that those clients will be referred on to the school counsellor.

Would you please complete the slip that .... may return.

Thanking you in anticipation.

Sincerely

...............................School Counsellor

....

I give permission for .... to understand work as a Buddy at Hampstead School.

Signed.. Date

Peer Buddies

Who are the peer buddies?
They are a group of 8 fellow students in year 13 who are available to talk to and support any year 7 students who are concerned about school, life, friends, family and relationships etc.

How will I know them?
Very soon a poster will be put in the year 7 room giving you information on the peer buddies and how you can contact them

Why should I talk to them?
You should only talk to them if you want to. They are a 'wicked' group of young men and women that we believe anyone would want to talk to – plus they have been trained to be peer buddies!

How do I contact them if I need to talk?
There will be a tutor group meeting in the near future where the peer buddies will join you to introduce themselves. Please feel free to chat to them!

An Emotionally Literate "Goodbye"

Student Name ....

Peer Buddying Certificate

.... SCHOOL

This is to certify that

....

attended .... hours (full course 24 hours) in Peer Buddy training, including Counselling Skills and Emotional Literacy Skills, at .... School

Date...............

Signed..

....

References and Short Bibliography

Author's Introduction, Para 4 line 3
"Certificate and Diploma courses in Emotional Literacy Development" courses run by Elizabeth Morris of the School of Emotional Literacy, Buckholdt House, The Street, Frampton on Severn, Glos, GL2 7ED

Preparation for the Programme, Para 5
"Guidelines for Counselling in Schools" BACP 2002, Page 7
"Counselling in a school takes place ....where children and young people can feel safe and comfortable. Ideally the room should be furnished in a way that creates an immediate distinction between the counselling room and a classroom or teacher's office. A secure place to keep case records and access to a confidential telephone line is also required."

The Programme, Page 9
Notes 4 and 5
"Guidelines….." BACP 2002, Page 7
"….children….need to have their whereabouts accounted for by means of appointment slip,"

Page 11
A day course run by The Association of Colleges of the Eastern Region (ACER)

The Programme, Page 12 Note 6
"Involving the students: a Peer Buddying Scheme" Young Minds Magazine 62 Jan/Feb 2003 Cathy Street and Jenny Svenberg "Room for improvement – adolescent views on inpatient care"
"Relationships with other young people on the unit were also discussed. This could be beneficial, giving mutual support.
See also:
Cowie and Sharp "Peer Counselling in Schools" (1996) David Fulton Publishers
"The adults often underestimate the capacity of young people to empathise with another's suffering and to offer helpful support and guidance."

Peer Buddying Pack

Page 49
The six conditions from Carl Rogers' 1959 seminal paper setting out his Therapy Theory.

Page 54
"Emotional Literacy Definition and Principles" and Session 7 "Emotional Literacy Skills Analysis" taken from course material, Elizabeth Morris, School of Emotional Literacy

Page 55
"Multiple Intelligences"
Definition taken from Howard Gardner (1993)

Page 56
"Skills Analysis" – taken from course material as on page 54.

Reading List and material invaluable to working in schools:

"Guidelines for Counselling in Schools" BACP 2002
"Clinical Counselling in Schools" Nick Barwick 2000 Routledge
"Peer Counselling in Schools" Heather Cowie and S. Sharp, 1996 David Fulton
"Nurturing Emotional Literacy" Peter Sharp 2001 David Fulton Publishers
"Frames of Mind" Howard Gardner 1993 Fontana
"The Multiple Intelligences" Howard Gardner 1993 Basic Books
"Developing Students Multiple Intelligences" Kirsten Nicholson-Nelson, Scholastic Professional Books
"TA for Teens" and "TA for Kids" Alvin and Margaret Freed, 1977 Jalmer
"Young Minds" bi-monthly magazine
"School Based Mediation Programmes" Richard Cohen/School Mediation Associates 1987 (USA)

School of Emotional Literacy

Since we started publishing in 2003 we have grown our library to over 30 publications, all of which have been written and designed by practitioners for practitioners. All our titles have been tried, tested and adjusted before going into print so that we are able to offer the very best tools to help you: tools which we know work, which are practical and which are readily accessible to any one who wants to help children fulfil their potential. We are always expanding our publications range because we are continually developing new resources to meet the demands of practitioners and to incorporate the latest research findings.

We can happily keep you up to date about new title releases by adding you to our mailing list, or you can browse our shop online at www.schoolofemotional-literacy.com where you can see everything we have on offer to help you.

If you visit our website you will see that our publications are not the only way in which we could support you. Our mission has always been to create the best chance for every child through the provision of a positive emotional education. From being the first organisation to bring materials for assessing emotional intelligence to Europe, more than 10 years on we now work in different countries across the world to support and train all the adults, whether they have a professional or a personal relationship, who work with children. We firmly believe that by developing children's emotional intelligence you ensure that they are more likely to be able to reach their potential in the widest sense, helping them to become well-rounded, creative, academically able, happy and socially adept people at the end of their schooling.

We offer training in a variety of forms to suit your individual needs, such as:

- Accredited Post-Graduate level Certificate, Diploma and Master's in Emotional Literacy Development

- Workshop days related to the practical applications of emotional literacy development, self-esteem building, supporting SEAL, behaviour management… and many more

- Train the Trainer courses in peer support, restorative practices and transforming relationships

- Conferences on all aspects of emotional literacy development

Above all, we are specialised consultants, experts in tailoring our services to suit our individual clients' needs. Being this flexible allows us to offer very effective recommendations to ensure maximum impact and sustainability.

If you would like more information on any of our services, then please feel free to give us a call or look at our website.

Other Publications

1. The Whole School Emotional Literacy Indicator by Elizabeth Morris and Caroline Scott
2. The Class Emotional Literacy Indicator by Elizabeth Morris and Caroline Scott
3. The Individual Emotional Literacy Indicator by Elizabeth Morris and Caroline Scott
4. Developing Social Skills – A Practical Solution by Elizabeth Scott
5. Build Self-esteem First – A Practical Solution by Athy Demitriades
6. Establishing a Counselling Service in your School – A Practical Solution by Emma Wills
7. I feel…. when….. Posters developed by Elizabeth Morris
8. Graffiti Feelings Posters by Claire McAleavy
9. Bullies aren't bad. An emotionally literate response to bullying by Heather Jenkins
10. 'SISTERS' Club Facilitators File by Annie Hamlaoui
11. Emotional Resilience Profile by Elizabeth Morris
12. Self Esteem Guidelines: developing a whole school policy by Elizabeth Morris
13. Face your Feelings Game by Liz Tew and James Bocot
14. Feelings Game by Heather Jenkins
15. IT'S OKAY TO BE ME by Annie Hamlaoui
16. The School and it's Counselling Service - a companion guide to "Establishing a Counselling Service in Your School - A Practical Guide" by Emma Wills
17. Multiple Intelligences in the Classroom: At-a-glance Guide to Assessing and Teaching using Multiple Intelligence Theory by Elizabeth Morris
18. Emotional Literacy Indicator for Early Years by Elizabeth Morris and Caroline Scott
19. More than 40 ways to develop emotional literacy in pupils by Elizabeth